# Ha! Ha!

## Steck-Vaughn.

HOUGHTON MIFFLIN HARCOURT

10801 N. Mopac Expressway
Building # 3
Austin, TX 78759
1.800.531.5015

Steck-Vaughn is a trademark of HMH Supplemental Publishers Inc.
registered in the United States of America and/or other jurisdictions.
All inquiries should be mailed to HMH Supplemental Publishers Inc.,
P.O. Box 27010, Austin, TX 78755.

**www.rubiconpublishing.com**



Associate Publisher: Wendy Cochran
Editorial Assistant: Dawna McKinnon
Creative/Art Director: Jennifer Drew
Senior Designer: Jeanette Debusschere
Designer: Gabriela Castillo
Cover image, title page–Shutterstock.com

James Proimos: "Bottoms Up" from MUTTON SOUP: MORE ADVENTURES OF JOHNNY
MUTTON, copyright © 2004 by James Proimos, reprinted by permission of Harcourt, Inc.
Michael Rosen: "The Hollywood" by Michael Rosen (Copyright © Michael Rosen 1988) is
reproduced by permission of PFD (www.pfd.co.uk) on behalf of Michael Rosen.

Printed in Singapore

ISBN: 978-1-77058-462-4
1 2 3 4 5 6 7 8 9 10   2016   21 20 19 18 17 16 15 14 13 12
A B C D E F G

# Contents

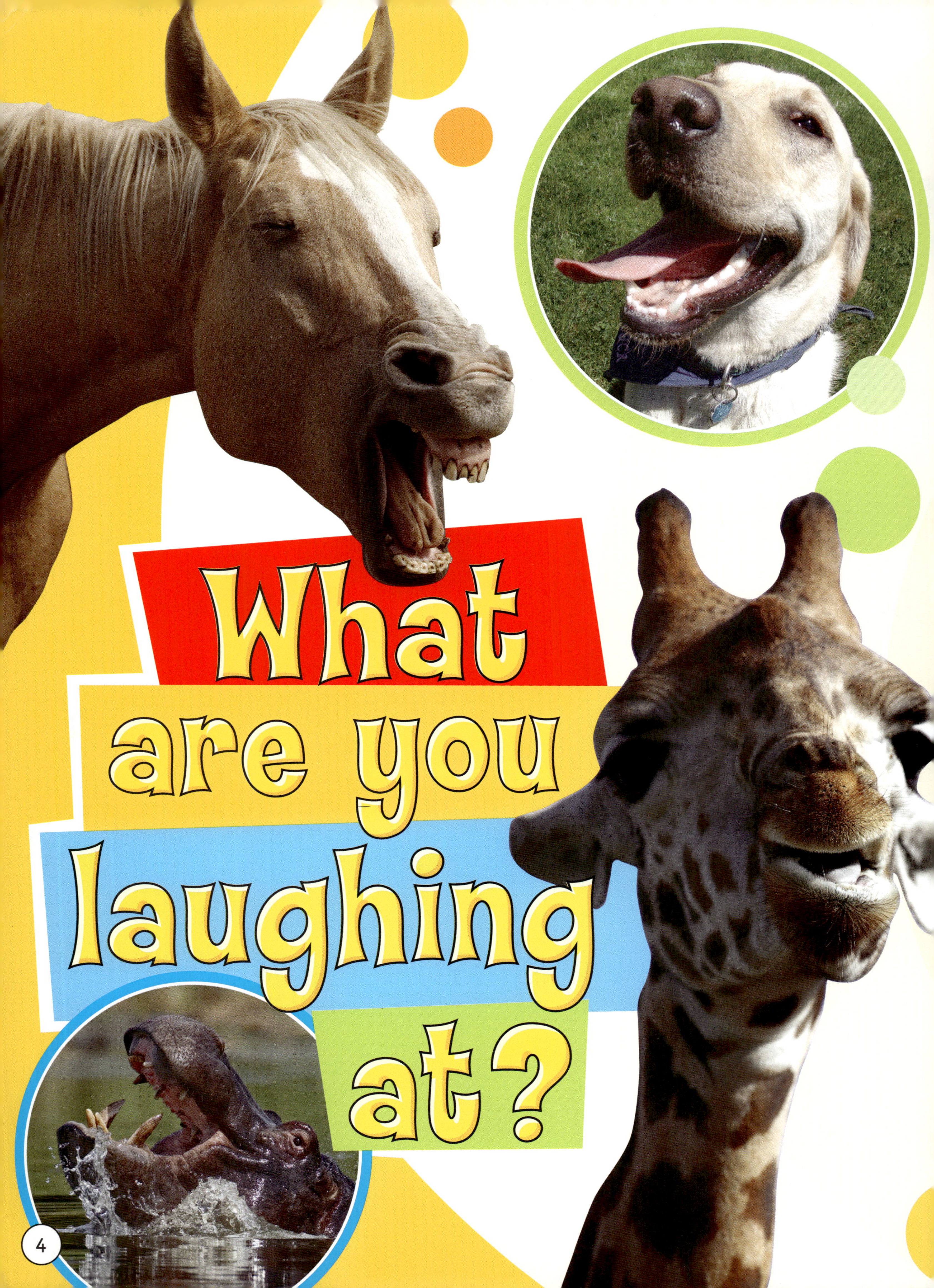

What are you laughing at?
4

# Recess Rhymes

Art by Maryann Kovalski

**A**s I climbed up
the apple tree,
all the apples
fell on me.
Someone shook them
and I know who.
The one
who did it
was
Y.O.U!

# I scream, you SCREAM, we all SCREAM for ICE CREAM!

## Who SCREAMS the loudest? YOU!

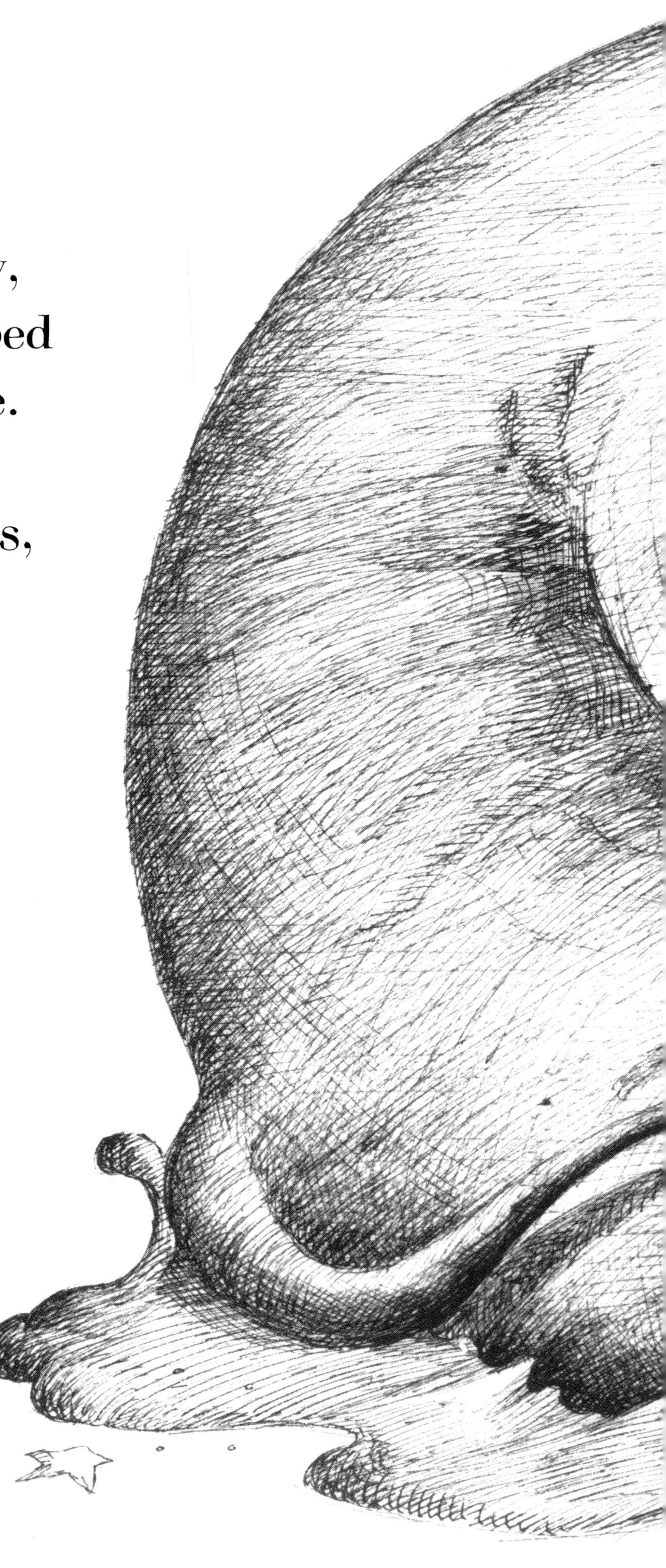

**W**ay down south
where bananas grow,
A grasshopper stepped
on an elephant's toe.
The elephant said,
with tears in his eyes,

"Pick
on
someone
more
your
own
size."

A peanut sat on the railroad track,
His heart was all a-flutter.
Along came a train — the 9:15 —
Toot, toot, peanut butter.

TOOT!
TOOT!
TOOT!
TOOT!
The end.

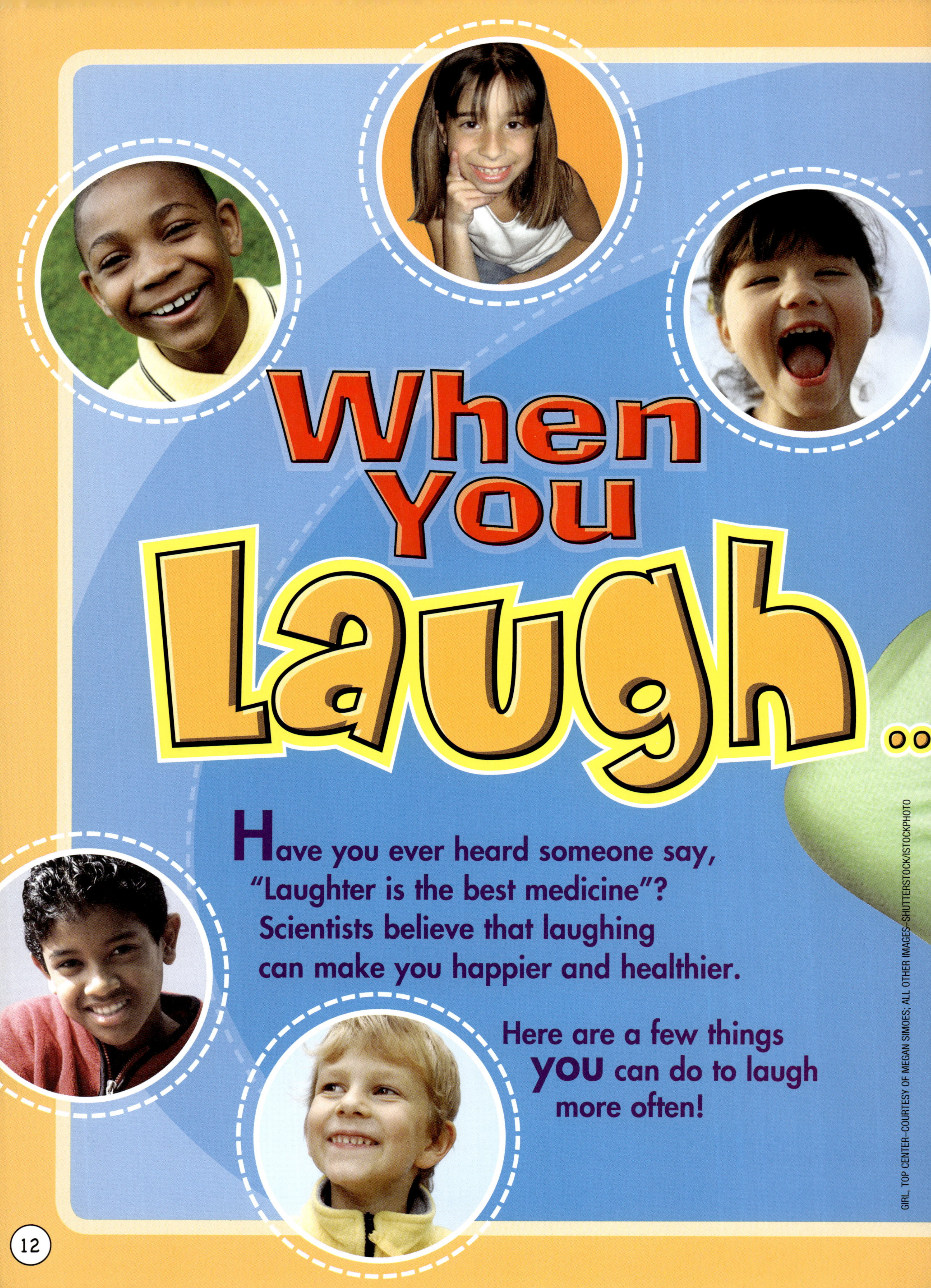

# When You Laugh...

**H**ave you ever heard someone say, "Laughter is the best medicine"? Scientists believe that laughing can make you happier and healthier.

Here are a few things **YOU** can do to laugh more often!

1 Make other people laugh!
2 Do silly things that make you laugh!
3 Make up your own jokes!
4 Have lots of funny friends!
5 Remember to laugh at yourself sometimes!

When You Laugh...
YOU'RE KIDDING!
Some funny facts about laughter!
ALL IMAGES—SHUTTERSTOCK
Try to tickle yourself!
Does it work?
14

Laughing gives your whole body a workout. It even works your leg and back muscles.

People often laugh when they hear others laugh.

Humans are one of the few species that laugh.

Laughing uses different parts of your brain.

The average adult laughs about 15 times a day. The average child laughs about 150 times a day.

People of different ages find different things funny.

You are more likely to laugh around other people than if you are alone.

The Hisser
The Giggler
Tee hee hee hee ho
Tee hee hee hee hee hee Tee hee
When You Laugh... HOW
SNG SNRT!
SNRT SNORT! SNORT!
The Snorter
The Silent Laugher
Art by Christopher Jones
16

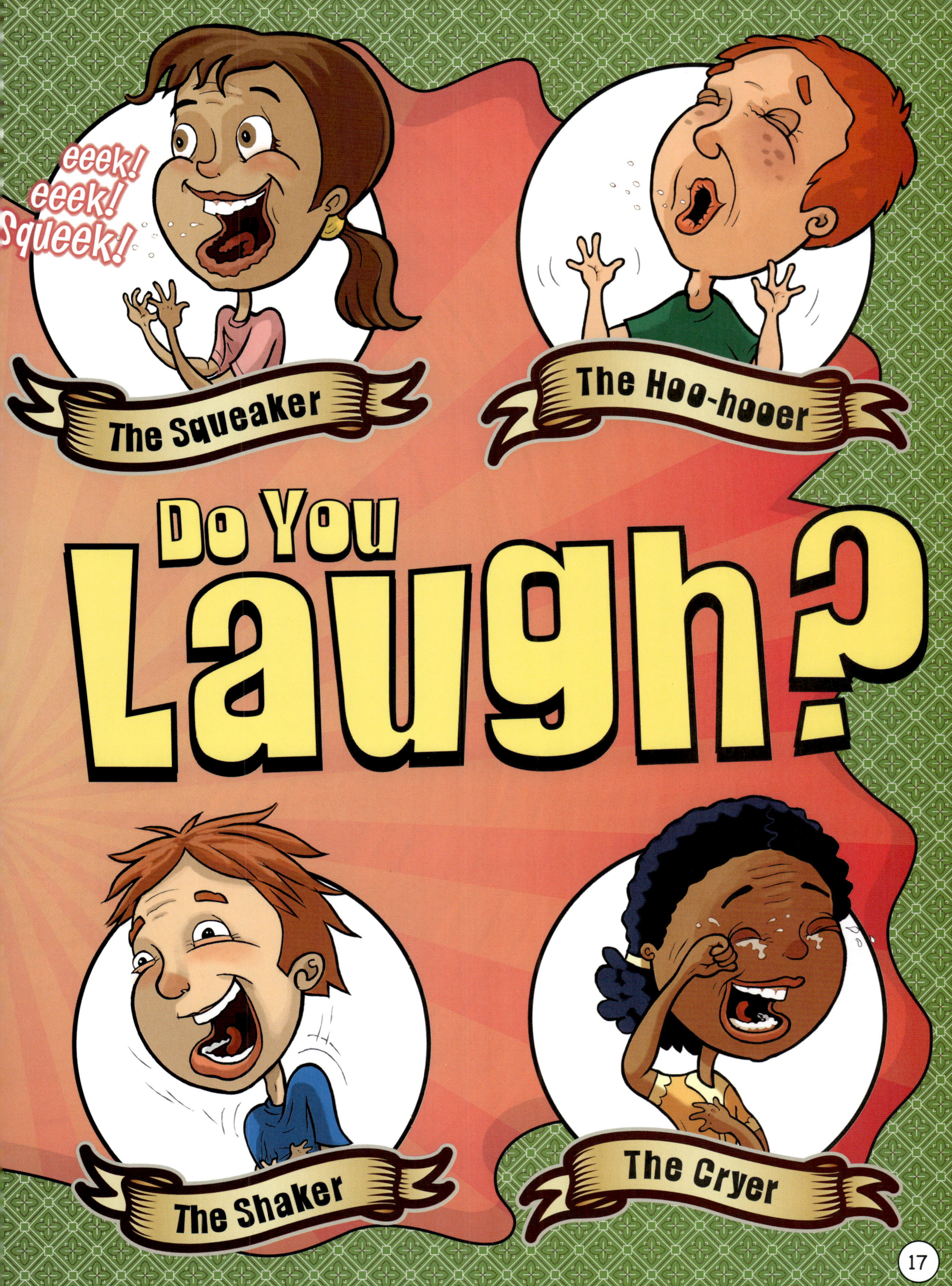

eeek! eeek! Squeek!
The Squeaker
The Hoo-hooer
Do You Laugh?
The Shaker
The Cryer

We went to this café,
and I had lots to eat.
I had fish and chips.
The fish was huge,
and there were hundreds of chips.
Hundreds and hundreds of them.

And I ate them all.

18

Then Mom asked,
"Anyone want any dessert?"
And we looked to see what there was.
There was apple pie.
Don't like that.
There was cheesecake.
Don't like that.
And there was ice cream.
I like that.

There was chocolate, strawberry, and vanilla.
I was just about to say,
"I'll have a strawberry ice cream,"
when I saw something else.
It said:
THE HOLLYWOOD.

And it was


The Hollywood
vanilla ice cream
peaches
cream
chocolate sauce
cherries
trifle
~ and ~
strawberry ice cream.

So I said,
"I'll have a Hollywood."
Dad said,
"He won't eat it.
They're huge."
But Mom said,
"No no no,
if he wants it, he can have it."
Dad said,
"Waste of money.
He won't eat it."
Mom said,

And we waited.

Then suddenly it appeared.
On its own.
Right in the middle of the tray.
With a little paper umbrella stuck in the top.
Everyone in the café looked round:
"What's that?"
"That's the Hollywood."
"Oh yes. That's the Hollywood all right."

And the woman put it down.
In front of me.
THE HOLLYWOOD.
With the little paper umbrella stuck in the top.
It was huge.
It was taller than me,
and I had this really long spoon
to eat it with,
and now
everyone was looking at me.

I had to reach up
to get the cherry on the top.
Got it.
In the mouth.
It was yummy.

Then on to the ice cream
and the chocolate sauce.
Dig in.
That was a bit rich but OK.

Dad loves ice cream and
chocolate sauce,
and he's watching me …
But I don't give him any.

Then there was some jelly stuff
And actually
that wasn't very good.
Actually —
It was horrible.

Dad said, "Slowing down are you?"
Mom said, "Leave him alone."

Then I got to the soggy cake.
That was even more horrible.
I couldn't bear it in my mouth.
I couldn't even put it in my cheeks.
I hunched my shoulders and
I spat some into my hand.
I stopped eating.

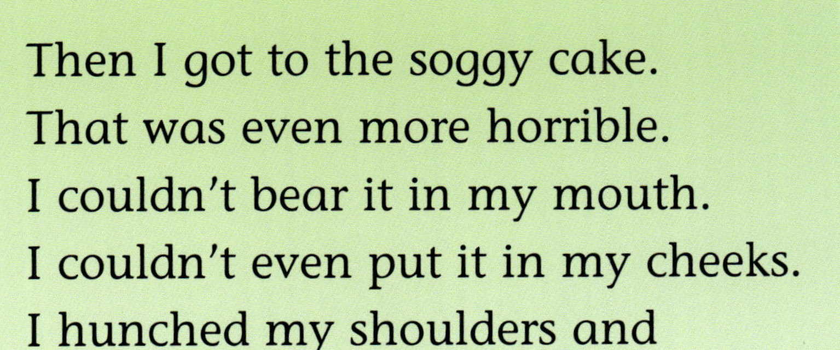

Dad said, "Stopped have you?"
Mom said, "Leave him alone."
"I don't like it very much," I said.

Dad's hand darted across the table.
"I'll finish it," he said.
You bet he said that.
"I'll finish it," he says.

And Mom turned to me and said,
"Never mind, dear.
You won't ask for one of those again,
will you?"
I don't think I will.

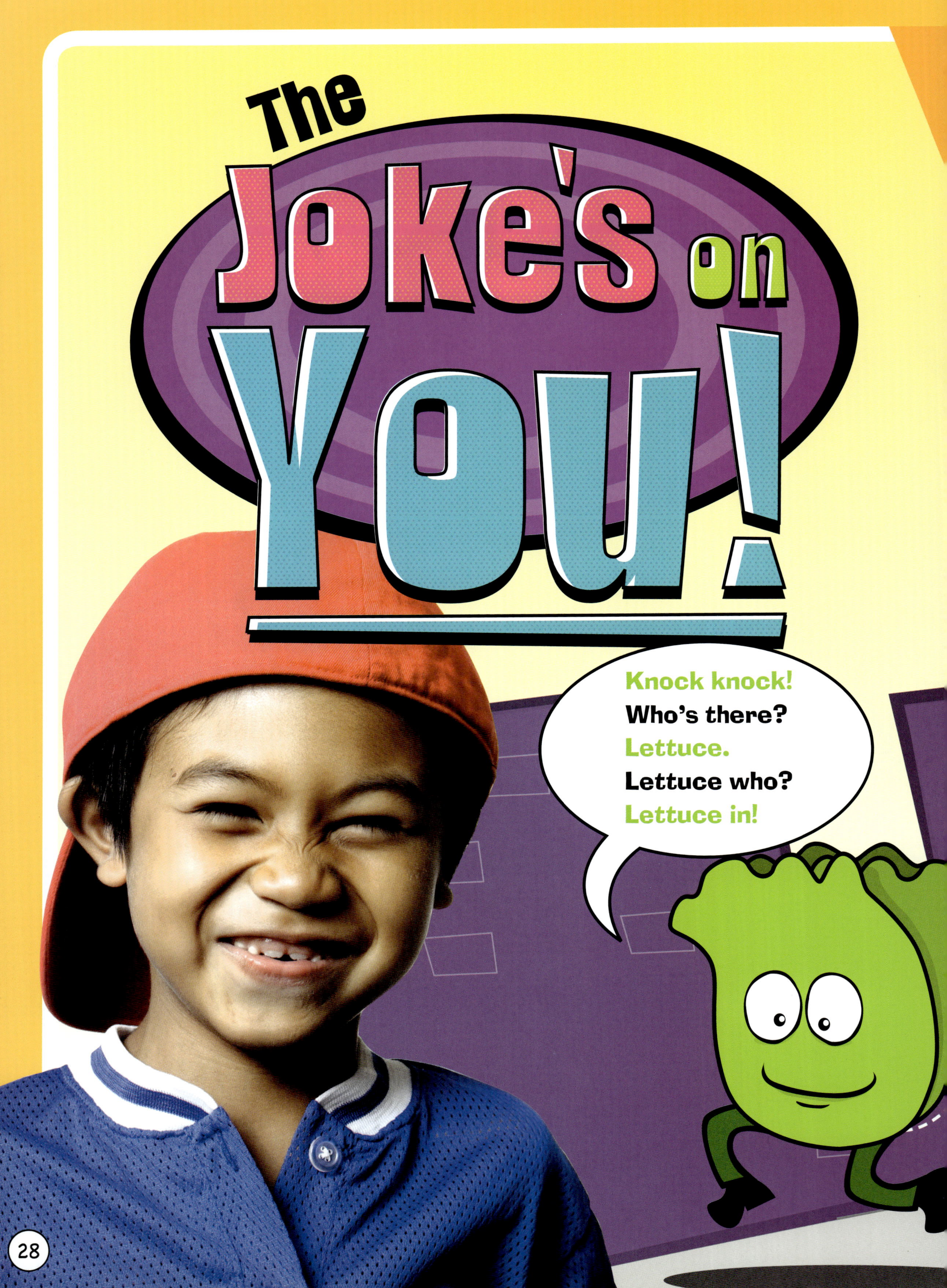

The Joke's on YOU!
Knock knock!
Who's there?
Lettuce.
Lettuce who?
Lettuce in!
28

# Knock knock!



**A** word that sounds like another word but has a different meaning can make a funny joke.

Knock-knock jokes follow this pattern:

# Silly Time

The trick to silly jokes is to ask a question and give a silly answer.

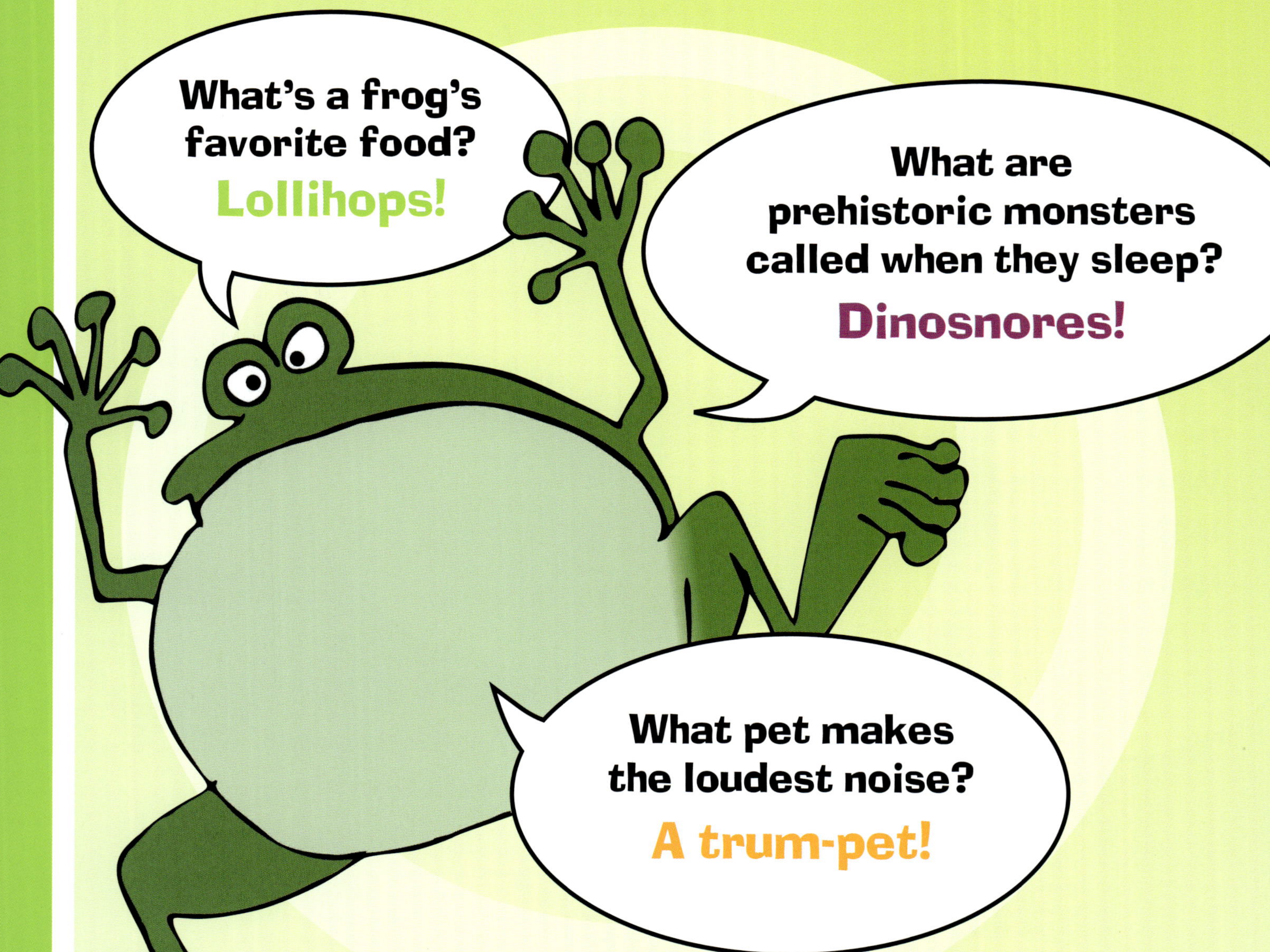

What's a frog's favorite food?
Lollihops!

What are prehistoric monsters called when they sleep?
Dinosnores!

What pet makes the loudest noise?
A trum-pet!

What's the best day to have bubblegum?
Chewsday!
What's an insect's favorite sport?
Cricket!
What happened to the cat who ate a ball of yarn?
She had mittens!

# Crossovers

**A**nother popular way to tell a joke is to follow the pattern: "What do you get when you cross …?"

What do you get when you cross a pig with an ambulance?
A hambulance!
What do you get when you cross a cat with an ape?
A cape!
What do you get when you cross a cow with a duck?
Milk and quackers!

# Tongue Twisters



Tongue twisters make people laugh. They are groups of words that begin with the same letters or have similar sounds.

Say each one of these ten times quickly!

Sixty-six
**sneaky** snakes

**A big black bug** 

Cheap **sheep** soup

A big **blue** bucket
of **blueberries**

**Toy boat**

# What do you call a ...?



**A**nother way to create a joke is to use this pattern: "What do you call a …?"

What do you call a boy with a dictionary in his pocket?
Smarty-pants!
What do you call a cat that you can rest your head on?
A cat-a-pillow!

# Bottoms Up

**By James Proimos**

Johnny always put his napkin on his head instead of in his lap.

He said "pronto" when he was supposed to say "please."

He hid Momma's plate whenever she left the table.

THIS JUST WON'T DO. I'M SENDING YOU FOR A LESSON WITH MS. BOTTOMS.
HER NAME IS MS. BOTTOMS? HA!

THERE IS NOTHING FUNNY ABOUT MS. BOTTOMS. SHE'S A MANNERS EXPERT.
DOESN'T THAT MAKE HER NAME EVEN FUNNIER?
KIND OF.

The next day Johnny went for his lesson with Ms. Bottoms.

GOOD DAY, YOUNG MAN.
PLEASED TO MEET YA, SISTA!
OH MY.

ONE HOLDS A TEACUP LIKE SO.
PINKY OUT

LIKE SO?

DON'T TALK WITH YOUR MOUTH FULL.
WHAT?

NOW, WHY IS YOUR NAPKIN ON YOUR HEAD?
IT LOOKED SILLY STUFFED UNDER MY ARM.

That was the last straw.

Ms. Bottoms took Johnny home.

That night at dinner,
Johnny was the perfect gentleman.
I AM SO IMPRESSED!
IF HE HAD A PINKY IT WOULD BE EXTENDED
CAN'T TALK. MOUTH FULL.
NAPKIN IN LAP
And it was fun.

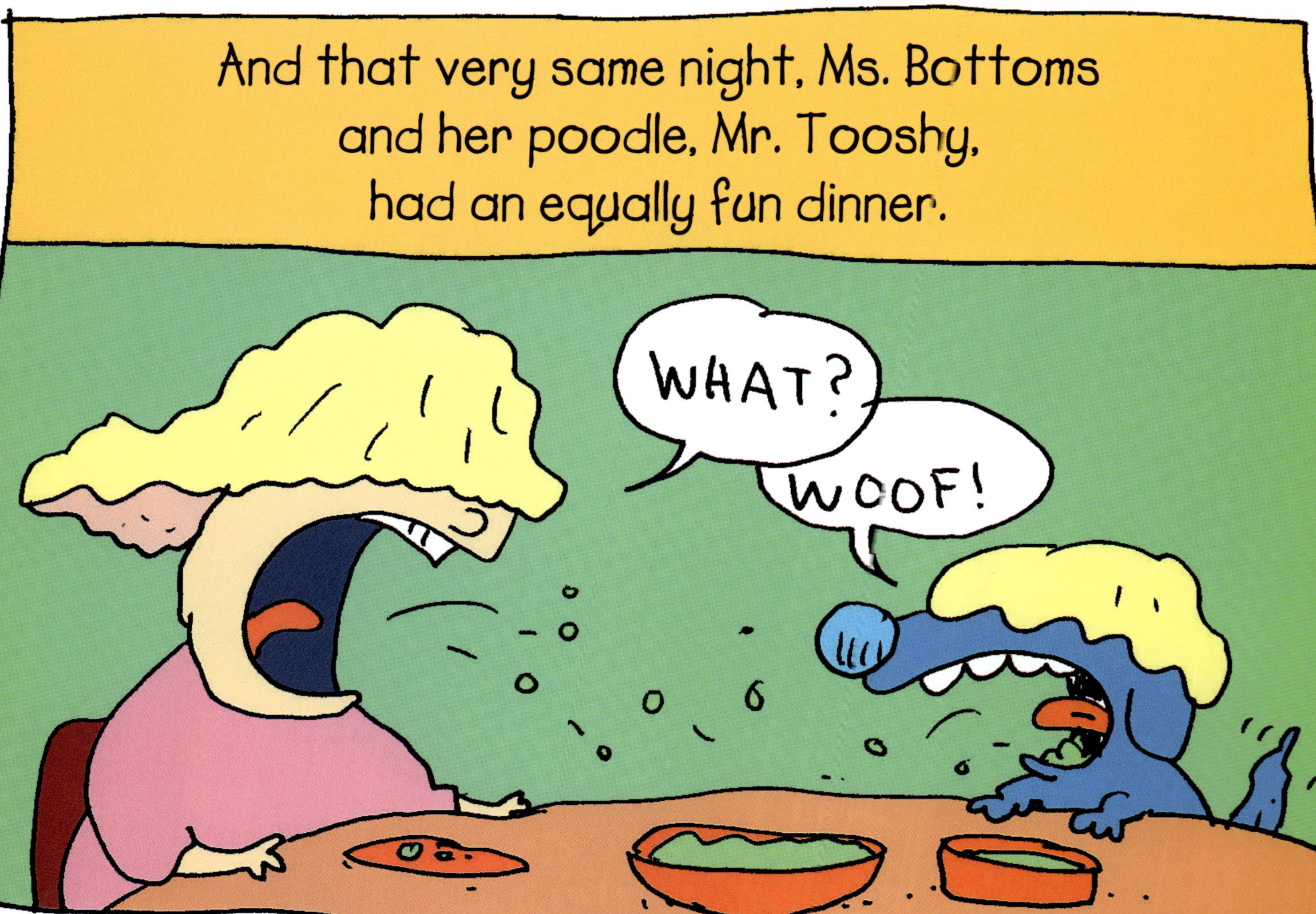

And that very same night, Ms. Bottoms
and her poodle, Mr. Tooshy,
had an equally fun dinner.
WHAT?
WOOF!

MUTTON
PUDDING HAS
NO LUMPY BITS,
BUT IT DOES
HAVE A CHERRY
ON TOP.

# Make Your Own FLIP BOOK

## Instructions

**YOU WILL NEED:**

- a pad of paper
- a pencil

1. Think of a simple image, like a smiley face or a ball.

2. Draw the image on the last page of your pad of paper. This will be the first picture in your flip book.

**3** On the page before that,
draw the same image
but make it move a little.

**4** Continue drawing the image
on each page,
moving from the back of the pad
to the front.
Remember to change the image
a little each time.

**5** When you are finished drawing,
hold the pad in your right hand.
Use your left hand to flip the pages
from back to front.
Watch the image move!

You can draw many things
in a flip book.
Here are a few ideas:
- a bouncing ball
- a person walking
- a ball going through a hoop
- a person making a snowman
- a person throwing a ball

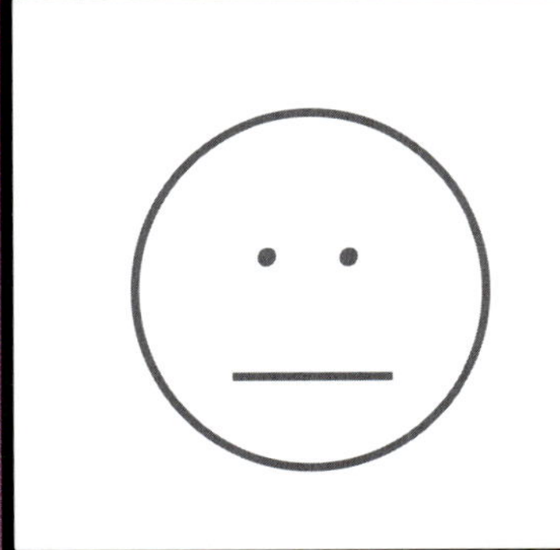

## High-Frequency Words

| | | | |
|---|---|---|---|
| along | eyes | grow | heart |
| more | own | pick | size |
| someone | tree | around | believe |
| best | body | child | different |
| does | even | few | friend |
| happy | hear | heard | laugh |
| often | people | things | time |
| use | whole | across | asked |
| couldn't | dear | else | everyone |
| fish | front | hand | leave |
| love | mind | never | please |
| really | right | turned | watch |
| woman | another | answer | begin |
| boat | broke | each | favorite |
| follow | groups | head | mean |
| six | sleep | sound | anything |
| close | home | instead | kind |
| left | name | next | night |
| nothing | same | talk | why |